IT'S TIME TO LEARN ABOUT APES

It's Time to Learn about Apes

Walter the Educator

Silent King Books
A WhichHead Entertainment Imprint

Copyright © 2025 by Walter the Educator

All rights reserved. No part of this book may be reproduced in any manner whatsoever without written per- mission except in the case of brief quotations embodied in critical articles and reviews.

First Printing, 2024

Disclaimer

This book is a literary work; the story is not about specific persons, locations, situations, and/or circumstances unless mentioned in a historical context. Any resemblance to real persons, locations, situations, and/or circumstances is coincidental. This book is for entertainment and informational purposes only. The author and publisher offer this information without warranties expressed or implied. No matter the grounds, neither the author nor the publisher will be accountable for any losses, injuries, or other damages caused by the reader's use of this book. The use of this book acknowledges an understanding and acceptance of this disclaimer.

It's Time to Learn about Apes is a collectible early learning book by Walter the Educator suitable for all ages belonging to Walter the Educator's Time to Eat Book Series. Collect more books at WaltertheEducator.com

USE THE EXTRA SPACE TO TAKE NOTES AND DOCUMENT YOUR MEMORIES

APES

Apes are special, big and strong,

It's Time to Learn about

Apes

They climb up trees and swing along.

With hands so clever, just like you,

They grab and hold and eat fruit too!

Some are tiny, some are tall,

Chimpanzees are not too small.

Gorillas big with mighty chests,

Orangutans in trees they rest.

No long tails like monkeys do,

That's how you tell an ape from who?

They climb with arms so strong and wide,

Swinging fast from side to side!

Apes are smart, they learn so well,

They use some tools, oh, can you tell?

A stick for bugs, a rock to crack,

They find their food with brains, not luck!

It's Time to Learn about

Apes

They talk with hands, their face, and sounds,

They hoot and howl and shake the ground.

Some can learn to sign and say,

What they need in their own way!

Apes love fruit and leaves to eat,

Bananas, nuts, and berries sweet.

They munch and crunch with mighty jaws,

And peel their food with strong, quick paws.

Mothers love their babies so,

They carry them wherever they go.

They teach them climbing, how to run,

And keep them safe till they are done.

They live in forests, wild and free,

In jungles thick with vines and trees.

Some roam the ground, some stay up high,

It's Time to Learn about

Apes

Some build their nests beneath the sky.

Apes are gentle, wise, and grand,

But need our help to save their land.

Their forests shrink, their food gets low,

We must protect them, help them grow!

Now you know, so when you see,

A picture of an ape like me,

You'll understand just what we do,

It's Time to Learn about

Apes

Apes are special, just like you!

ABOUT THE CREATOR

Walter the Educator is one of the pseudonyms for Walter Anderson. Formally educated in Chemistry, Business, and Education, he is an educator, an author, a diverse entrepreneur, and he is the son of a disabled war veteran.
"Walter the Educator" shares his time between educating and creating. He holds interests and owns several creative projects that entertain, enlighten, enhance, and educate, hoping to inspire and motivate you. Follow, find new works, and stay up to date with Walter the Educator™

at WaltertheEducator.com

www.ingramcontent.com/pod-product-compliance
Lightning Source LLC
LaVergne TN
LVHW052017060526
838201LV00059B/4065